The Poetry
Of
My Life

Lost Loved Ones

By Marie Romano

ISBN: 9780988554306

Dedicated to the heroes
and tragic heroes of my
life
for without them
I would not see...or be.

The greatest thing a human being ever does in this
rld is to see something...To see clearly is poetry,
prophecy and religion, all in one."
(John Ruskin)

Table of Contents

<u>Preface</u>

This book is a compilation of poems that I had written from 2011 to 2012. It was soon after my mother's death in March 2011 and leading up to my daughter's wedding day on May 27, 2012. There were so many mixed emotions that had come to surface during that time. It would appear that loss had triggered those feelings. The loss of my mom and then the loss of my daughter in a different way. In my menopausal state, I began to reflect on all the lost loved ones who are no longer here and who would be absent on my daughter's wedding day. I came to realize their importance in my life, then and now. They are my heroes and tragic heroes. Writing has been extremely therapeutic for me. This is the poetry of my life.

<u>My Mom…Where My Life Began</u>

When I was born my mom was brought to tears
So I have heard through all my years
Having suffered three miscarriages before me
I was named, the "Miracle Baby"

Her only daughter brought her much joy and glee
My younger years we played with Barbies
Having been the only girl amongst three brothers
I only had my dear mother

As I became a young girl
My world began to swirl
Through all the good and the bad
I had become very sad

As I was inappropriately touched
I was damaged as such
These things were not spoken about much
This became my crutch

My mother's loving arms
Couldn't keep me from harm
At the young age of eight
I felt so scared and betrayed

My mom did not know how to communicate
And she seemed depressed from day to day
Much to my dismay
I no longer knew how to play

I was too young to know
Exactly what she was going through
As a teenager, my mom seemed distant
She was no longer listenin'

She was preoccupied
As her marriage had died
When I became engaged to be married
She seemed so very happy

She loved Peter with all her heart
Who knew then, he would be the first to part
He was like a son to her, most would agree
She conversed more with him than with me

My mom and I had an estranged relationship
It has been quite a trip
As I grow older
I have become less colder

I have grown to understand like no other
About this woman I called mother
When I became a mother-to-be
I vowed not to be like she
A fate that had its own destiny

She was an awesome nanny
That would be understated to many
She went above and beyond for her grandchildren
They were her life,
It was like having her own children all over again

My mom loved to dance and sing
More important than anything
Halloween and Valentines
Is what made her chime

Some would say she was a bit naïve
But she was happy, so it seemed
She was unrealistic and lived in the past
She loved watching old movies and loved the casts

As her children and grandchildren grew older
She began to smolder
As she thought she was no longer the most important person in the
lives
Instead of realizing they were all just living life

She sat daily by the phone just waiting for someone to call
It was her ALL
She never stopped giving
But at some point she did stop living

Her last and final years
Brought me to tears
As dementia had set in
I felt so much compassion

It was sheer torture to watch her demise
Her death was no surprise
It was a blessing in disguise
As there was no more life left in her eyes

Since her death I understand my dear mother
Like no other
I have become like her for this is true
Despite my trying not to

She was a humble and simple soul
Someone who I am proud to have known
I have inherited her poetic trait
And I have been on a roll as of late

I had the unpleasantness of going through her stuff
And as if that was not enough
I found birth certificates and death certificates
Of the four siblings I never knew
She had a lifetime of suffering, for this is true

I read the early love letters between her and my dad
Which I have found to be so very sad
As I then found the hate letters after their divorce
Who knew love could take such a dreadful course

As happy as my mom appeared to be
There was a sadness inside her deep
All I could do was weep
Her life seemed as if she was mostly asleep
To avoid her pain and grief

Today as I stand
I have a new plan
I no longer fight my heredity
I have learned to embrace it 'til eternity

As corny as I may now be
I am just a leaf on my family tree
I am grateful for all she taught me
As I have now begun to see

<u>My Dad...The First Man I Loved</u>

I came into this world with a head full of curls
I was branded, "Daddy's Little Girl"
Right from the start
I had stolen his heart

It was love at first sight
He was the first man in my life
I can recall sitting on his lap or his knee
He was always with me

As a young girl I was told
By my dad, "I wish there was some magic pill
to stop you from growing old"
I thought he was crazy at the time
Until I had two daughters to call mine

He liked to tease
I would get upset with ease
He and my brothers enjoyed playing ball
I had no choice but to join them all

My oldest brother spent the most time alone with him
As he would at times grin
He was an only child for several years
When I came along, I brought him to tears

As my brother grew into a young man
There was a plan
Camping and fishing they went
So many wonderful times they spent

Ten years after my oldest brother was born
My dad had two more sons to call his own
Three sons my dad had
He sure was proud and glad

My dad was thrilled to have had twins
It was hard work again and again
My dad was much older than before
These little boys he adored

He was proud of us all in one way or another
Some thought he was only proud of Jim, the doctor
He loved John's creativity and sense of humor
And George will always be his namesake and first- born

I spoke to my dad daily
We always had something to say
I cherish our times together by the water
I truly loved being his only daughter

Some would say he favored me most
But there were times that I felt lost
He was a father to me and my brothers of three
But there was another side to him that I did not see

He had some bad habits, to which I ignored
To me he was my dad without any flaws
I loved him unconditionally
As I continued through life blindfully

He was my best friend 'til the end
My mentor and confidante
He enabled me
But I could not see

There is a fine line between helping and enabling your child
This took me a long while
To fully understand the damage caused by this man
I now had to learn how to stand

The day my dad died
Was possibly the worst day of my life
Watching him take his last breath
Right before his sudden and tragic death
I did not know what to do
I had no clue

I now feel grateful for having been with him that fateful night
As I was with him as he began his final journey and flight
His passing was quick and he did not suffer
I loved him like no other

I have learned so much since then
And I revisit that day every now and again
Through sorrow and pain
I have so much to gain

I miss him as much today as the day he left me
The only difference now is that I can see
I have learned to embrace the pain that resides within me
As he will always be a very special part of me

Peter...My First True Love

We first met in high school
I thought he was so cool
He picked me up in his red Road Runner car
I learned so much about Mopar

He loved his muscle cars, no doubt
It was sad when his Road Runner got rubbed out
It wasn't long before he got a Chevelle
A cracked "A" frame damned it to hell

I can remember our first date
It was very late
When he drove me home from St. Finbar's Bazaar
In his suped up red car
He handed me a car air freshener and said
"I think we would make a good team"
As his eyes gleamed

He seemed to be a simple guy
Good morals for sure, this was no lie
He was a bit old fashioned
And lived life with passion

We hung out back in the day
When eight track tapes played
"Rumors" was the number one album that summer
Going back to school was a bummer

He was my prom date
I graduated in nineteen seventy eight
He got his GED in nineteen eighty two
It is never too late, for this is true

We were engaged by nineteen
Thinking back now, we were just teens
We grew up together and looked forward to growing old
Who knew then what was to unfold

Our future looked bright
And we started with such might
We married at twenty
Life seemed plenty

He was a carpenter by trade
A living he chose to make
He was proud as he could be
When it came to projects of wood and concrete

e was a musician who played the drums, saxophone and clarinet
He was so very talented
He was an artist too
He could draw and paint like no one I knew

The Beatles were his favorite band for sure
He truly loved this "Fab Four"
George Harrison was his favorite band member
From what I can remember

He loved the great outdoors
He loved to camp and make smores
He was a hunter of deer
When he found his prey he would cheer
He enjoyed guns, rifles and target shooting
Bows and arrows too

He was a Yankees' fan
And a Cinncinati Bengals' fan
He enjoyed his sports
Mainly baseball and football of sorts

He cherished his family and friends more than anything
And was ecstatic when there was a gathering
He thoroughly enjoyed the holiday seasons
Good company, food and wine were the reasons

He truly was unique
As he continued to speak
With an "old-world" sense
He saw life through a different lens

He enjoyed making wine with his uncle or just hanging with me
As he felt it was time well spent
He cherished his memories of yesteryear
And at times wished he could go back there

At twenty-four
Our first baby was born
It was a daughter
Who made our eyes water

She was the apple of his eye
That was no lie
She could do no wrong
As he played her songs

Two years later, our son arrived
Peter cheered, then cried
We were never bored
We now had two children not to be ignored

Our boy
Brought so much joy
Peter could not wait to buy him toys
Cars, trucks, balls and Legos

When our son was three
We added to our family tree
Another daughter to see
She brought us so much glee

Another little girl
Our life was a swirl
Two daughters for him to love
And a son to be
Just like he

We were now a family of five
Our home was our hive
We enjoyed our children as much as we could
Trying not to let life's troubles interfere, like we should

He loved to read from the "Golden Books"
It was all it took
And all that mattered
As he played "Candy Land" or "Chutes and Ladders"
He also taught them things back then
That perhaps he shouldn't have

Such as how to clean a gun or a rifle
To him it all seemed a bit trifle
Or how to skin a dead deer
Which brought the kids to tears
He then proceeded to show them
How to saw off a limb

He thought nothing of making a pig roast out in the yard
To some he seemed barbaric or odd
They loved their dad
He was all they had

As time moved forward, our troubles began
Financial difficulties were not in our plan
Many unkind words were said
Not cool for our kids to hear before bed

Towards the end
We were less than friends
As we didn't always see eye to eye
And at times he made me cry

There is a fine line between love and hate
But I stuck to my vows, he was my mate
I love him with all my heart
It was devastating when we did part

When he was killed by a drunk driver on that fateful day
The shock and rage that came
Made us all age
That day set the stage
For all that followed
I for one, in sorrow and pity, wallowed

He was a healthy, young man who was strong as an ox
Maybe he should have been more sly like a fox
As a young widow I stood
Without a clue, as I became unglued

We were together for twenty-seven years
And to this day, I am still brought to tears
This wasn't in our plans
I now had to take a stand

I have learned to live with my pain
For suffering has led to my living again
As my daughter's wedding day came near
I thought of all of our years

It saddened me to think that he wouldn't be here
To take our daughter by the hand
To give her away
In the traditional way

I had to watch as I stood at the altar
As another man escorted my daughter
He was the closest person to Peter
Which made it easier
With much love and hope
She did glow

There is no replacement
And our hearts will always ache for him
As time moves forward, I continue to grow
As I have learned so much from all that I now know

This will never go away
From it I have learned to take the time to play
No matter how much time goes by
I will at times hurt for my children and cry

Pain and suffering have enlightened me
In ways that are unimaginable for most to see
Peter will continue to be
A very special part of me
My life today wouldn't be
If it weren't for he

My Other Father

My other dad
Whom I was fortunate to have
Was as warm-hearted as can be
He always aimed to please

He was a funny guy
I, at times laughed 'til I cried
He was a hard worker
Husband and father of three boys
He brought so much joy

When I was seventeen years old we met
I was his pet
I was the daughter he never had
Boy was he glad

Over many years we had grown
Into a true father and daughter, who would have known?
He was there for me always
And came by my home every day

He was never nosey
But knew that my life was not always rosey
He truly cared about me mostly
As some decisions were costly

He and his first-born son were inseparable
They at times were incapable
Of seeing eye-to-eye
But they did try

Work and play
Kept him busy day-to-day
We thought he was here to stay
Never thought he would be taken away

He was an amazing grandfather too
There was nothing he would not do
He enjoyed buying them donuts at any given time
He would have stopped on a dime

He loved taking my son to get another patch
For his Boy Scout uniform
And my girls melted his heart
Right from the start

When he became ill
Life stood still
For thirteen years he suffered
For that there was no buffer

Congestive heart failure was his claim
It at times made him lame
In and out of hospitals for so many years
Brought me to tears

He lost his fight
One fateful night
He died in his wife's arms
He was no longer feeling harm

He was only sixty-seven years of age
And never reached that "golden years" stage
He is so terribly missed
I remember that good-bye kiss

Life is not the same today
I cherish yesterday
I could not have asked for a better dad
His memory leaves me feeling fortunate and glad

<u>My Aunt Mary</u>

My Aunt Mary has been a mentor to me
An inspiration to so many
I have never met a woman with so much heartache
She always accepted what came her way

She managed to maintain her sense of humor
Perhaps, that is what kept her sane
She was one funny lady!
Her facial expressions alone
Would make you laugh
As you knew exactly what she was thinking

My aunt had a lot of nervous energy
She would stay up all night cleaning or wallpapering
I remember my sleepovers with my cousins
She would stay awake and tuck us in under the covers

Another thing I remember
Was the twenty-fifth of December
When she would dress all four of her children
In matching Christmas outfits
She loved Christmas!

My aunt was a hard worker
She worked in the city up until her cancer diagnosis
She was there on 9/11 and saw it all
But even then she did not fall

She was a survivor in so many ways
I admire her strength and endurance today
My aunt lost her parents at a very young age
That set the stage

She married my uncle when they were young
And raised a family of two daughters and two sons
She became widowed too soon
With raising teens to continue

Cancer became our family curse
To my uncle she was a nurse
Years later her son was diagnosed
She felt so lost

I can remember her making giant vats of herbal teas
For these two members of my family
She became a nutritionist at home
With her smiley face she never groaned

My Aunt Mary would whip you up a meal
And always made you feel
Welcomed in her home without a second look
She was a phenomenal cook

My aunt was a doting mother
She would do anything for her children
Without it being a bother
Even after being stricken with cancer

She was an amazing grandmother!
She truly loved life simply
She just wanted to be surrounded by family
Without becoming a burden

When my aunt became a millionaire
She did not change one bit
"We Are Family" became her skit
She walked around the neighborhood
Like the rest of her neighbors

She refused any and all special treatment
Her first trip to Atlantic City, as a millionaire
She sat at the penny slot machines
She was just too precious!

Her children, grandchildren and great-grandchildren were her lif
She was a mother, aunt and wife
She was sincere and dear
In all my years
She never once forgot my birthday

It saddens me that she did not live long enough to enjoy her weal
One cannot put a price on health
She was never materialistic in any way, shape or form
She was just the norm

She was wealthy in a different way
She found her wealth in her family from day to day
Her children are now her legacy
They have and will continue to make her proud

Saying goodbye is a difficult task
But at least I had the chance
To say how I felt
As I knelt
At her beside
Trying not to cry

She had the softest skin
Porcelain white in color
And the most beautiful blue eyes
Up until her demise

My Aunt Mary will live forever in our hearts
I will cherish the times we shared
And the conversations of care
I will continue to learn from her

My wish is that she is no longer suffering
And is now at peace as her new journey begins
My aunt will be forever loved and missed!
She was truly one in a milllion!

<u>My Aunt Arlene</u>

I will never forget that call
As I can recall
That my aunt had died
"Too young", I sighed

I did not understand God's plan
Here one day and gone the next
At fifty-two
Who knew

A brain aneurysm took her life
She was a loving mom and wife
She was an aunt and a friend
I wished her life had not ended

She was always there to advise
As we were neighbors, she did apply
Her knowledge of pool care
And her fruit and vegetable garden

I learned so much from her
This woman could muster
As I am now her age
I cannot imagine leaving this stage

Because of this wonderful lady
I am extremely grateful to be here today
My Aunt Arlene may have left the scene
She will live forever in my memory

Dead at Twenty-nine

Dead at twenty-nine
Was a dear friend of mine
Best friends from the start
She will forever be in my heart

From doll carriages
To marriage
And let's not forget
Those crazy teen years

A car accident is how she died
This childhood friend of mine
I remember the shock and how I cried
As I was in disbelief that she had expired

At such a young age
She never got to the next stage
Leaving me grateful for today
As death can come on any given day

Her parents have recently joined her
I cannot imagine the pain they had endured
They are now together again
I imagine in a place called heaven

I think of her often
And truly miss my friend
We survived the best and worst of times
I am grateful for the memories left behind

It has been a long road since then
One that I revisit every now and again
It has led to my enlightenment
For knowledge has been sent

I now know how
To survive
And stay alive
In order to thrive

I have since met a new man
He is my best friend
And soon to be my new husband
My first husband will always be
A part of us three

From my hurt
I had a growth spurt
Of another kind
Which is so very hard to find

My pain and grief I now own
For without them I could not have grown
I have learned to embrace it all
I no longer feel small

I never felt embarrassed
I felt more harassed
This is now my past
A memory to forever last

A slight reminder of how people could change
Myself included, I will never be the same
I am grateful not to have succumbed
I have returned to the role of being a mom

<u>Not Goodbye, So Long</u>

It was not by choice you left me
This I see
That day you died
I lost a big part of me

For better or worse
Those were our vows
Til death do us part
Tell that to my heart
To which you will always be a part

A part of my past
That will forever last
You live through our children
They are proof of our undying love
You are now my angel up above

We grew up together
And so much did we weather
Growing old was not in the plan
You were a unique man

As I prepare to marry again
It is time to let go
This I know
For I have found a new love
With whom I hope to grow old

For thirty-three years I bared your name
Things will never be the same
It is time for a change
As I continue to live my life
As someone else's wife

This is not goodbye my love
So long for now
My childhood sweetheart, friend
Husband and father of my children
Until we meet again

<u>Sophie…My Pugly</u>

The day we met I still can recall
She was so tiny and small
Unlike my dogs before
Which were so big and tall

She was somewhat ugly
This pug of mine
But cute in her own way
She was the funniest dog I ever had, I must say

She became my companion and friend
'Til the end
I will never forget, soon after I became widowed
How she sat beside me
During those lonely days and nights

I will forever cherish our walks
By the water
And to the park
She seldomly barked

As she grew old she became ill
And then blind
From diabetes
Followed by uncontrollable urine and feces

This is the part I hate
Of being a dog owner to date
Saying goodbye
As I prepare for her to die

A decision I dreaded for a while
She sure did make me smile
And now all I can do is cry
This is no lie

I will forever hold her close to my heart
As we part
I am grateful for the times we shared
I will miss her being here

As she died in my arms
There was a sense of calm
She looked so beautiful and at peace
I felt at ease

She will now join my other dogs
My canine loves
Wherever they may be
Princess, Alfie and Casey
They were more like family

Dogs definitely become family members
Life without them I cannot remember
I cannot imagine my life without them all
As they have brought so much love and joy as I can recall

The love is unconditional
A love that is hard to find
Saying goodbye
Makes my cry

www.ingramcontent.com/pod-product-compliance
Lightning Source LLC
Chambersburg PA
CBHW031343040426
42443CB00006B/454